Original title:
The Peace Lily's Promise

Copyright © 2025 Creative Arts Management OÜ
All rights reserved.

Author: Arabella Whitmore
ISBN HARDBACK: 978-1-80581-813-7
ISBN PAPERBACK: 978-1-80581-340-8
ISBN EBOOK: 978-1-80581-813-7

## Resilience in Green

In the corner stands a plant, so bright,
With leaves like arms, ready for a fight.
It wobbles a bit, but don't you fret,
For in its heart, there's no regret.

Each droplet of water, a playful dance,
It stretches high, given half the chance.
A little bit bent, but always bold,
With a tale of laughter waiting to be told.

## Petals of Quiet Hope

Soft petals whisper secrets in the air,
A silly plant with a humorous flair.
When morning sun tickles its face,
It giggles softly, keeping grace.

A dance in the breeze, just out of sync,
It sways to the rhythm, not a moment to think.
With roots so strong and a wink so sly,
It promises joy, oh my oh my!

## Vows of the Silent Guardian

In the muted glow of the evening light,
Stands a guardian, ready to delight.
With a giggle and sway, it takes its stand,
Promising smiles across the land.

It's a protector with a cheeky grin,
Bound to keep the blues from creeping in.
So if the world feels heavy and gray,
Just give that flower a wink and sway!

**Nature's Gentle Assurance**

Leaves waving like they just don't care,
A floral comedian with charm to spare.
It nods and bows, like it's on a stage,
Offering comfort, wisdom, and sage.

In a world so loud, it hums a tune,
With petals that dance under the moon.
A gentle reminder, fun and spry,
Nature's own joy, lifting spirits high.

## A Journey Through Still Waters

In a pot where silence reigns,
A plant sways without any claims.
It knows the secret of being cool,
Reclining like a wise old fool.

Leaves nodding in gentle breeze,
Whispering jokes of the buzzing bees.
Water's dance, a splash of cheer,
Tell me now, is there a beer?

### The Surrender to Tranquil Hues


Colors blend in soft embrace,
I see a grin on every face.
This sight could make a frown dissolve,
Even the grumpiest can't evolve.

Petals flutter, wearing bright smiles,
Tickling shy hearts for a while.
In tranquil moments, laughter rings,
Who knew peace could sprout such things?

## The Quietude Within

In corners where giggles reside,
A plant thrives, not needing to hide.
It chuckles softly as it grows,
In the stillness, silliness flows.

Whispers around, but no loud shouts,
Comedies bloom where laughter sprouts.
So here's a toast to calm delight,
Where every leaf tells jokes at night.

## Blooming in the Stillness

In gardens where the humor's ripe,
A bloom awaits, no need for hype.
With every gaze, a giggle puffs,
While ants parade in tiny tuff.

The roots reflect some quirky glee,
Its petals wave, 'Come laugh with me!'
In funny silence, joy takes flight,
To bloom in stillness, pure delight.

## An Oath to Everlasting Calm

I swear by the soil, soft as a hug,
My leaves wave hello, no need for a shrug.
When life gets all messy, and troubles arise,
I'll bring you sweet smiles and plant-shaped goodbyes.

So let's dance with the breeze, just you and me,
I promise to flourish, just wait and see.
With petals so pure, we'll share some delight,
In a world of giggles, we'll bloom through the night.

## Harmony in Delicate Form

In this jungle of chaos, hear my decree,
I vow to be tranquil, just follow my lead.
With roots dug in deep, I stand tall and proud,
A whimsical plant amidst a wild crowd.

If your worries are heavy, come sit by my side,
We'll chuckle at troubles, watch them slide.
With a wink of a leaf and a nod of a petal,
We'll share silly secrets, let laughter be settled.

## The Guardian's Touch

With a leafy embrace, I guard your peace,
In times of confusion, my joy will not cease.
I'm here with a grin; no frown will survive,
Let's giggle at chaos, together we thrive.

A shield made of green, I'll keep worries at bay,
With humor and love, I'll brighten your day.
As we frolic through whispers of soft, gentle breezes,
We'll create a calm space where laughter just pleases.

## Unfolding Whispers of Light

In a world of bright colors, I'll twirl in delight,
My petals will shimmer, dazzling in light.
With a wink and a twirl, I'll dance on the sill,
Who knew that a plant could bring such a thrill?

As shadows grow long, and the sun starts to fade,
I'll burst into laughter, no need to be afraid.
Join me in joy, let each moment take flight,
Together we'll sparkle, like stars in the night.

## A Canvas of Quiet Reflection

In the corner it stands, quite still,
With leaves like a tiny green grill.
It waves in the breeze, a sight to behold,
Whispering secrets, both shy and bold.

Dust bunnies frolic, uninvited guests,
But the flower just laughs, never stressed.
Photosynthesis? Such a fancy word,
It just sunbathes while looking absurd.

At night when the moon plays peek-a-boo,
It sways gently, turning skies blue.
A statue of calm in a world of haste,
My leafy friend, a green-coated taste.

**The Stillness Beckons**

Hush now, the plants are plotting again,
They giggle and scheme like cheeky men.
My flower just sits, thinking it's sly,
While the dust gathers, oh my, oh my!

A tiny throne in its leafy domain,
It rules over chaos with nary a strain.
When I water it, it feels like a spa,
Yet complains about care like a diva, ha!

Cousin Cactus pokes fun from the sill,
But it knows, the lily's got charm and skill.
Together they plot for the next sunny day,
While I just laugh at their leafy ballet.

## **Nature's Gentle Resolution**

In a sunny spot, it takes the stage,
Like an actor on set, no need for a page.
With every new leaf, a quiet cheer,
Kind of like finding your lost favorite beer!

It dances in drafts, sways left and right,
What are you doing? Oh, just feeling bright.
A throne of tranquility, that's the plan,
While I try not to spill my whole can!

It blushes with pride when water descends,
Like it's at a party with all of its friends.
Growing taller and taller, no end in sight,
Who needs a ladder when you're this light?

## The Dance of Undisturbed Petals

Petals poised gracefully, a jig and a twirl,
While I sit and watch this leafy swirl.
Its dance is a marvel, oh what a sight,
Like a flower in rhythm, embodying light!

"Watch me," it seems to shout with glee,
"Forget your worries, just look at me!"
I snicker and say, "What's your big secret?"
"Just chill, my friend, don't make it a feat!"

Nature's comedian, a true master of jest,
Whispering laughter that simply won't rest.
In this oasis where humor's a must,
We laugh at our troubles, it's love and trust!

## A Prelude to Reflection

In the corner, a plant so shy,
Hiding from the sun up high.
It whispers jokes, a secret cheer,
Blooms like laughter, oh so near.

Dancing leaves in the gentle breeze,
Tickling toes, oh, what a tease!
It nods along to silly tunes,
Bringing giggles, bright as moons.

## The Bloom of Soulful Stillness

With petals poised like a fashion show,
Staying calm, putting on a glow.
It winks at the dust, laughs at the dirt,
Swirling joy in skirts of shirt.

A comedian in a pot so small,
It knows the punchlines, has them all.
With every bloom, a jester's grin,
Nature's way of pulling you in.

## **Veils of Serene Light**

In the morning light, it takes a bow,
Waving to friends, come see this wow!
Chasing shadows, dreary and grey,
With a smile that steals the day.

It plays peek-a-boo with the sun,
Whispers 'Stay', oh what fun!
A little chat, a twist of fate,
Who knew plants could be so great?

## In the Lap of Nature's Grace

Sipping rain, it starts to sway,
Telling tales in a leafy play.
Mimicking sighs of passing cars,
Underneath the watchful stars.

It checks its makeup in the dew,
Polishing leaves, it's true, it's true!
With each glance, it steals the show,
Making sure we all know how to glow.

## Nature's Whispered Secrets

In the garden, blooms so bright,
Plants gossip in morning light.
A fern tells tales of ageless woe,
While daisies dance in a daisy show.

The roses blush with sweet delight,
As tulips tease, with colors bright.
A squirrel snickers, the cheeky thief,
While daisies snort—fall's just brief!

Butterflies swear they saw a bee,
Who claimed it's allergic to honey tea.
The gardener trips, laughs on a vine,
And even the weeds know how to shine!

So plants unite, in whispers soft,
With jokes and jests that lift them aloft.
A tranquil vibe, with laughter free,
Nature's secrets, all just to see!

## Tranquility's Embrace

In the stillness, where silence frolics,
A cactus jests about its prickly topics.
A willowy friend sways with glee,
"Don't mind the stares, everyone loves me!"

Amidst the blooms, a lawn chair sighs,
As a lazy bumblebee just flies.
It lands on a petal, with heavy grunts,
"Life's too short for work, let's do stunts!"

The pond reflects a giggling frog,
He croaks out jokes—it's a comedy blog.
With each little splash, he brings the cheer,
"Hey folks, where's the party, is it here?"

So nestled within this vibrant space,
Nature's charm wraps in a warm embrace.
The world outside can buzz and race,
But in this haven, laughter finds its place.

## Unseen Hands of Comfort

A wise old tree, with branches wide,
Offers shade to squirrels who glide.
"Bark less, have fun!" it seems to say,
As acorns gather for a silly play.

Bumblebees buzz, telling tall tales,
Of honey adventures and sweeter trails.
"Don't fret", they buzz, "it's never bleak,
Just follow the scent, and have a snack sneak!"

A hidden turtle winks with charm,
"Slow and steady! No need for alarm.
Life's a journey, not a race,
Let joy be the goal, be a slow-paced ace!"

In this realm where all seems bright,
Laughter blooms in pure delight.
Unseen hands weave comfort near,
In nature's heart, there's naught to fear.

## In the Shade of Serenity

Beneath the trees where shadows gleam,
Nature giggles, it seems a dream.
A chipmunk twirls, a furry ballet,
Laughing at weeds that try to play.

Leaves rustle softly, sharing the joke,
A dandelion puffs with every poke.
"Blow me away!" it cackles in cheer,
As wind carries dreams, drawing all near.

In this cozy nook, all worries cease,
Ladybugs clink, enjoying their peace.
"Drink in the moment," they chirp in delight,
In the shade of serenity, everything's right!

So here we'll laugh, in nature's embrace,
Finding joy in each silly space.
With whispers that softly lead us here,
Together we'll thrive, year after year.

## The Quiet Heart's Repose

In a pot sits a lovely plant,
Waving to me, it seems to chant.
"Close your eyes, take a light breath,
I promise you'll escape the stress!"

With roots that twist and leaves so bright,
It whispers secrets, pure delight.
"Chill out, my friend, don't you despair,
I'm here to make you stop and stare!"

Its flowers bloom like laughter's sound,
Each petal spinning joy around.
"Leave your worries, take a seat,
Let's dance along to this heartbeat!"

So when the world feels loud and rough,
Just chat with me, it's never tough.
We'll sip some sun and dream awake,
For peace is found in each heartache.

## Simply Blossoming Peace

In my room, a green friend thrives,
Wearing pants of leaves, it jives.
"Hold still, dear world, come share my space,
This calmness wears a funny face!"

The sun rays giggle as they gleam,
Tickling leaves like a cheerful dream.
A little breeze that sways my chair,
Entices smiles into the air.

I tell the plant my silliest joke,
It sways in response, gives a poke.
"Life's a hoot, don't take it grim,
Just look at me, I'm sprouting whim!"

So here we sit, in laughter's trance,
A goofy duo, taking a chance.
With every leaf, a chuckle shared,
In simple joy, our hearts are bared.

## A Timeless Invitation to Calm

Come gather 'round my leafy friend,
Who knows how to laugh and just pretend.
"Let's chill awhile, don't rush too fast,
For silly moments are meant to last!"

With petals like pillows, soft and sweet,
It beckons all who pass its seat.
"Why worry when you can just drift?
I'm here to share life's most precious gift!"

And in its shade, giggles abound,
Where tranquility and humor are found.
"Life's just a game, so play it right,
Let's enjoy this peaceful flight!"

In a cozy nook, we spin strange tales,
Of dancing squirrels and dreamy snails.
With every chuckle, calmness reigns,
As laughter dances amidst the plains.

## Underneath the Canopy of Grace

Beneath the leaves, a world so grand,
Where happiness blooms, oh so planned.
"Let's brew some giggles, stir up delight,
For peace, my friend, is always in sight!"

With spiraling vines and a cheeky grin,
It invites all to join in the spin.
"Worries fade like a puff of smoke,
While we bounce through life's gentle stroke!"

Each flower jokes, "What's green and bright?
A plant in a thinking hat, what a sight!"
It chuckles back, with a mighty sway,
"Come laugh with me, it's a peaceful day!"

So under this canopy, we all shall rest,
In a joyous lull, it feels like a jest.
Together we'll breathe, relax, and play,
For laughter grows better with each sunny ray.

## A Gentle Promise to the Soul

In the corner, a plant takes a stand,
With a leafy grin, it's well-planned.
Whispers of joy, its petals unfold,
A comedian in green, with stories bold.

It tickles the air with its quirky pose,
Leaves waving like hands, for laughs it flows.
With soil so rich, it reigns supreme,
A jester of nature, in a leafy dream.

Beneath the sun, it leans for a hug,
Like a playful child, or a snug little bug.
In its serene dance, troubles take flight,
As humor blooms in the soft, gentle light.

So here's to the plant with a heart so light,
Making us chuckle, with pure delight.
In this funny world, it finds a niche,
A promise of peace, with laughter to preach.

## Petals Laced with Hope

In a vase, a flower, quite the wise fool,
Winks at the people, who think it's cool.
With petals all lined, like a net of dreams,
It giggles and shimmers in soft, sunny beams.

It sways to the beat of a whimsical tune,
Reminding the house they'll dance to the moon.
In its company, gloom refuses to stay,
With a chuckle, it banishes gray away.

Each day it promises a little more cheer,
With a laugh in its leaves, it draws everyone near.
A laugh-out-loud blessing, in every sprout,
Who knew hope could be a fun little bout?

Petals of joy, laced with delight,
Bringing a smile, morning and night.
In its vibrant charm, we're never alone,
Our funny green friend, always at home.

**Nature's Whispering Embrace**

A plant on the sill, with a grin quite wide,
In a soft, leafy voice, it wants to confide.
With each crooked leaf, it nudges good vibes,
And gardens of laughter, where nature subscribes.

Its whispers take flight, on a warm, playful breeze,
Telling all passersby, to smile with ease.
Like a stand-up comic in a petal-clad suit,
It spins funny tales, oh, how they compute!

With roots deep in joy, it's hard to resist,
A charm like a joke, that twirls and twists.
In every small bud, there's a giggle, a cheer,
Bringing colors of laughter, so bright and near.

So let's raise a glass to the flora around,
In jokes only plants know, true joy can be found.
A promise of peace, wrapped in a jest,
Nature's embrace, truly the best!

## The Tapestry of Serenity

In the garden of giggles, a flower shines bright,
With tales of delight and pure silly light.
Each petal a punchline, each leaf a big jest,
Creating a tapestry, happiness blessed.

A nature-bound artist, with humor in bloom,
With every new leaf, it chases the gloom.
It dances in sunshine, it twirls in the rain,
Each chuckle it offers, a soothing refrain.

The world spins fast, yet this plant won't budge,
With jokes in its roots, it holds a tight grudge.
Against all the worries that flutter in haste,
In its smiley embrace, there's no moment to waste.

So gather around for a laugh or a cheer,
With petals that promise to always be near.
In this funny arena, where serenity sways,
It weaves us together in joy-stitched displays.

## Unveiling Inner Peace

In a pot, she stands so proud,
Her leaves whisper soft and loud.
A smile blooms, but just a tad,
When dust collects, oh, isn't that sad?

She sways to tunes of morning light,
Dancing slowly, what a sight!
A quirky plant, with roots so deep,
Her promise made, no time for sleep.

With watering can, I hum and sing,
She sways and jiggles, what a fling!
Her petals smile, in hues so bright,
Feeling fabulous, oh what a delight!

When friends come over, they just can't tell,
If it's her peace or my jokes that sell!
Together we laugh, in our little nook,
Outside the world, it's our vibrant book.

## The Pact of Pure Radiance

In the corner, she makes a pact,
To shine so bright, with no exact act.
Her leaves, they sparkle, like glittery dreams,
Giving hugs, or so it seems!

I promised her water, she gave me a grin,
In our little dance, that's how we win.
With each drop, she giggles and gleams,
Turning my living room into sunbeams!

She teases the cat, with shadows so sly,
"Catch me if you can!" she dares with a sigh.
In the dance of the day, antics abound,
Who knew peace was so joyfully crowned?

Strange reflections in the window pane,
Both plant and I are quite insane!
But laughter binds us, a quirky thread,
In our peaceful world, we dance ahead.

## Tides of Gentle Assurance

She whispers gently, with each slight breeze,
Promising laughter, with utmost ease.
A wink and a nod, she knows my ways,
Carrying me through the silliest days.

Whenever I stumble, she shakes her head,
"Water me later, go play instead!"
Her leaves bounce back, like old pals in glee,
In this watering game, I find my spree.

"Sunshine's my enemy!" she often exclaims,
While basking in warmth, but dodging the flames.
With quirky demands, she's quite the delight,
Each day a new riddle, each night a slight fright!

But together we laugh, through leafy dreams,
Finding joy in the silliest schemes.
For even in peace, we bring the fun,
A plant and a friend, shining like the sun!

## Secrets of a Flourishing Heart

In cheerfully green, she smiles so wide,
With secrets of laughter tucked deep inside.
Her petals giggle, in a joyous dance,
Inviting my presence, a quirky romance.

Peeking from soil, she raises her brow,
"Am I not cute? Come on, take a bow!"
With every sprout, she tells her tale,
Of hopes and dreams, on a grand scale.

With a spritz and a twirl, we thrive in glee,
Turning the mundane into jubilee.
Through ups and downs, we share the part,
In this jungle of life, we've found our art.

Sipping laughter from a teacup bright,
She sparks my soul, like dancing light.
In our little world, secrets impart,
A flourishing plant, a ticklish heart.

## **Drops of Tranquil Assurance**

In a pot with a grin, it sits so proud,
Leaves waving hello to the sunlight crowd.
"Water me, but don't drown," it seems to say,
Full of calm and a twist on a sunny day.

With friends like the ferns who are always late,
It giggles at weeds, claiming it's first rate.
"I'm the zen master of your little space,
Breathe me in, and find your happy place!"

Tiny droplets fall, like soft little tears,
As it whispers sweet nothings, calming your fears.
A dance in the breeze, it's quite the delight,
Chasing worries away, oh what a sight!

So here's to the green that's sneaky and sly,
With its leafy charm, it'll help you fly.
In the wild world of chaos, it stands so still,
A jester in green, with a heart to thrill.

## The Quiet Offering of Nature

In a corner of rooms where chaos can dwell,
The green comes to play, but shh, don't you yell!
It offers a giggle, a sigh, and a cheer,
With petals that whisper, "I'm always here!"

With sunlight as friend, it stretches so wide,
A natural jester, with nowhere to hide.
Its humor is subtle, but oh so divine,
Giving peace with a smirk, it knows you'll be fine.

In its leafy cocoon, laughter takes flight,
As it winks at the root, "You're doing alright!"
Each bloom, like a joke, makes you chuckle with glee,
While it stands there all wise, sipping tea with a bee.

As the day rolls along, and worries do loom,
Just peer at this plant, watch it fill up the room.
With promises soft, it holds out its hands,
Inviting you in to its peaceful demands.

## A Soft Promise on the Breeze

Dancing in sunlight, it sways to and fro,
Whispers of calm seep from roots down below.
Its leaves like a heart, plush and alive,
It pulls out a grin, invites you to thrive.

With a grin ever wide, it drapes down like hair,
A jester of flora, spreading joy everywhere.
"I'll lighten your load, make your worries all flee,
Stay close, little friend, and just trust me!"

Each droplet of water is like a big hug,
While it tickles the air, a soft little shrug.
Nature's own joker with roots that might tease,
This plant is a treasure, an expert at ease.

So heed well the message, from petals so bold,
It's laughter in green, with stories untold.
With a wiggle and giggle, it brightens the night,
A soft little promise that all will be right.

## In the Company of Gentle Blooms

In a lush little corner, a gathering blooms,
They chuckle and smile, pushing back the glooms.
Leaves outstretched wide, they throw a grand ball,
Whispers of fun echo through the hall.

They tease the shy shadows that linger near walls,
Throwing petals like confetti to nature's grand balls.
Held in their laughter, a mischief so dear,
With soft little secrets that only plants hear.

Bright colors flutter, and giggles abound,
As they revel in moments, no worries are found.
Swaying and prancing, they dance in delight,
Creating a scene that feels ever so right.

So raise a small toast to the greenery's grace,
To joyous arrivals in this bustling space.
With the company gathered, life sparkles and blooms,
In this quirky assembly, love chases the glooms.

## Embrace of Silent Grace

In the corner, a refuge lies,
With green leaves that reach for the skies.
It sways not in storms, but with humor instead,
Whispers of laughter escape from its bed.

Potted with care, it stands so proud,
Listening to secrets, never too loud.
Its blooms like a wink, a cheeky delight,
Hints at adventures that dance in the night.

Roots in the soil, a jester at heart,
With every new sprout, it plays its part.
Embracing the joy, it teaches us all,
To find giggles and glee, even when we fall.

So here's to the plant with the softest grace,
A master of calm in this bustling place.
Let's laugh with the leaves, in our own little space,
Finding joy in the chaos, a beautiful chase.

## A Covenant of Calm

In a trim little pot, a soft promise lay,
Not to disturb, but to brighten our day.
It shimmies and sways, a dance so refined,
While chaos around, it's perfectly aligned.

Its friends are the dust bunnies, cheeky and bright,
Sharing their tales late into the night.
While others may fret, it lets out a sigh,
With petals of wisdom that tickle the sky.

In this room of giggles, it anchors the fun,
A truce with the world, as bright as the sun.
Promises made, with each playful breeze,
Bringing calm to the chaos, with effortless ease.

So let's raise a glass to this whimsical friend,
Who knows how to laugh and help us transcend.
In the madness of life, it's fun that we seek,
With petals of cheer, it speaks without speak.

## Petals of Hope

A beacon of joy in a room full of gloom,
With petals like smiles, it fills every room.
Let's party with green, as it giggles along,
Whispering melodies, a jolly old song.

When the clock strikes twelve, it's still shining bright,
Polishing dreams in the soft moonlight.
Dancing like crazy, it nudges us near,
With each little bloom, it spreads warmth and cheer.

Its leaves are the life coaches, wise and absurd,
Sending us signals without uttering a word.
Where worries once loomed, it lights up the space,
With just a soft chuckle, a warm, leafy grace.

So here's to the petals, a smile in each hue,
Bringing light into shadows, it's fun to pursue.
A joyful companion, it winks with delight,
Promising sunshine, all day and all night.

## The Guardian of Stillness

In a world that spins with a comical spin,
Stands a gentle watcher, let the fun begin.
With a nod to the chaos, it keeps a straight face,
As if to say, 'Breathe, you're safe in this space.'

Leaves like a shield, guarding bright laughter,
Surrounded by giggles, forever thereafter.
It cracks a good joke, dripping with grace,
As we all gather round, like a warm embrace.

A sassy little plant with a twinkle and grin,
Its petals a promise to let love in.
So when trouble knocks with a clatter and fuss,
It's the guardian here, counting each "just us."

So let's roll in the joy, in a green leafy dance,
With whispers of laughter, it offers a chance.
To pause for a moment, and truly embrace,
The humor of stillness—our silly safe space.

## Heartbeats in Blossom

In a pot so green, a friend does dwell,
With leaves so pure, they weave a spell.
Her roots tickle ground, feeling quite spry,
She winks with a leaf, oh my, oh my!

A dance in the breeze, like a hip-hop star,
While sunbeams shiver, she raises the bar.
Calm in her heart, she giggles with glee,
"Don't water me too much, or I'll float like a sea!"

With petals all bright, like an artist's feast,
She teases the cats, igniting their beast.
In a room full of laughter, she keeps quite the beat,
With a twist and a turn, she's the life of the street!

Her whispers of joy in the quiet of night,
With humor and charm, she makes the world bright.
So here's to our friend, the leafy delight,
In a garden of giggles, let's hold her tight!

## Unfurled Dreams of Stillness

A plant of such grace, in a corner she stands,
With dreams in her leaves, and life's little plans.
A shushy hush hero, she takes on the task,
"Can you believe the drama? Just don't ask!"

Her friends in the air want to join in the fun,
They spin and they sway, under bright, glowing sun.
With roots deeply planted, she's just here for laughs,
"I swear I'm not grumpy; just dodging the gaffs!"

When raindrops do tickle, she giggles and glows,
"Bring on the sunshine! Just no more snow woes!"
She sways like a dancer, each leaf knows the score,
In her calmness, she hides a sweet, silly roar!

In the lull of the night, she dreams boldly wide,
Crafting wild stories that tickle her guide.
So watch her unfold, with a wink she'll declare,
"Life needs a punchline, so please, spare a chair!"

## Tides of Calm Amidst Chaos

In a world full of noise, she takes a cool stand,
With petals so poised, as if made by hand.
A jester of green, she sways like a pro,
In chaos, she chuckles, "Just go with the flow!"

When rumbles of thunder dance heavy on air,
She giggles and twirls, a humor so rare.
"I've seen storms, my friend, got leaves for a shield,
Bring on your tantrums; I refuse to yield!"

With drops from the sky, she's bathing in fun,
"Water me lightly, let's dance in the sun!"
She's got all the charm of a whimsical sprite,
In the heart of the chaos, she holds her light.

So here's to the plant in her playful zone,
With jokes in her roots, she's never alone.
Celebrate mayhem, with laughter unite,
For in nature's buzz, she's our delight!

## Surrender to the Serene

In a corner, so happy, serene and quite bright,
A flower does giggle, bringing bliss in the night.
Her petals a whisper, "Let's chill and relax,"
In a hug from the sun, she just leans and stacks.

With a soul like a balloon that floats with a cheer,
She rumbles with joy, "My friends, gather near!"
"Life's too short for frowns, let's laugh at the breeze,
A dance for the ages, let's shimmy with ease!"

She knows all the secrets the night tends to keep,
With roots deep in laughter, she doesn't lose sleep.
When storms roll in worry, she's still feeling fine,
"Let's throw a party, all the stars can align!"

So here's to the plant that promises cheer,
With a joke in each leaf, she's the friend we hold dear.
In a world full of chaos, she reminds us to sing,
"Let's embrace the absurd; it's the best kind of thing!"

## **Whispers of Serenity**

In a corner, it sat, lush and bright,
Its leaves waving, giving delight.
I asked it for a cup of tea,
It winked and said, "Just brew with glee!"

Yet there it stood, still and calm,
Listening to my tales of qualm.
A plant with secrets yet untold,
I wondered if it might unfold.

"If only I could share a joke,"
I laughed, as people stared at smoke.
"Do you know why the bush won't hide?"
"Because it's not the leafy type!"

So here we are, an odd pair,
A plant so wise, yet strange as air.
With roots in soil, it still finds grace,
In this ridiculous, leafy place!

## **Blooming Beneath Shadows**

Beneath the eaves, it starts to sway,
With unkempt charm, it steals the day.
"How do you grow without the sun?"
It chuckled back, "It's all in fun!"

Sipping raindrops in its bowl,
While watching cats, oh what a goal!
"I once saw a dog with big, floppy ears,
He looked at me and brought me cheers!"

"I bet I'm happier than a fig,
While you're all lost in your own gig.
I dance with breezes, laugh with shade,
Your worries fade, I've got it made!"

It blooms with laughter, heart on sleeve,
Crafting joy, no need to grieve.
So raise your glass, my leafy friend,
Let's celebrate, and never end!

## **Embrace of Tranquil Waters**

Nestled near a bubbling brook,
It kept a watch, just like a rook.
"Ever tasted water, oh so fresh?"
It asked, as if it were a chef!

"I'm not a fish, but what's the fuss?"
I said, and caused quite a fuss!
"You're funny, dear, I must agree,
But think of all the fish that see!"

Brushing slow, the lily swayed,
In its cool realm, worries laid.
"Do you think a fish tells tales?
Or does it simply swim and sail?"

The water chuckled all around,
While the plant giggled, lost and found.
With lively tales of watery fun,
They danced together, one and done!

## A Gesture of Soft Light

In the window, bright and proud,
The soft light made it laugh out loud.
"I shine like stars, just wait and see,
But no one takes my selfies, whee!"

With petals bright, it cut a joke,
"You think I'm fancy? Well, it's no hoax!
I'm just a plant, no big degree,
Yet here I am, all eyes on me!"

Chasing dust motes, high in the air,
"Can you believe it? They stop and stare!
They think I'm wise, with stories to weave,
Little do they know, I just achieve!"

It danced in rays, a beauty rare,
With cheeky smiles, beyond compare.
So here's to joy, in every bloom,
Bringing laughter to every room!

## In the Shade of Serenity

In sunlight bright, I hide my face,
With leafy arms, I claim my space.
A watering can, my liquid gold,
In my embrace, you'll never fold.

Come sit with me, we'll sip some tea,
I'll spill the secrets of the bee.
Whispers dance through gentle leaves,
In my calm, the heart believes.

Frogs croak songs from ponds nearby,
As dragonflies go zipping by.
I nod and wave, I'm not too shy,
A plant of joy, oh me, oh my!

So take a seat, no need to race,
In this fine spot, we've found our place.
With laughter lush and tranquil air,
Life's worries fade, no need for care.

## **Blossoms of Reassurance**

A tiny sprout with big old dreams,
I take my time, or so it seems.
With petals plump, I gleefully sway,
A giggling friend, come out and play!

Potting soil, oh what a mess,
I've dirtied hands to great excess.
But in the muck, I find my cheer,
My floral jokes bring all the tears.

I chat with bugs who pass on by,
They laugh with me, oh my, oh my!
In this garden, joy's the key,
A leafy heart is wild and free.

So grab a trowel, plant your dreams,
In colorful shades of sunny beams.
Together we can bloom and grow,
A comedy show in the garden's glow!

## The Language of Pure Tranquility

In whispers soft, my leaves converse,
With humor light, they break the curse.
A gentle breeze, a chuckle shared,
In leafy tongues, no one's scared.

"Why did the plant refuse to dance?"
"Because it felt too root-bound, just by chance!"
We giggle hard, our stems entwined,
With laughter here, stress is maligned.

The sun sets low, a comical show,
As shadows stretch in evening flow.
I trade my puns with buzzing bees,
Their little dances put me at ease.

From every petal, laughter spills,
With every bloom, I share my thrills.
In my quiet world that's ever true,
A riot of joy, just me and you!

## **Echoes of a Soft Horizon**

When morning breaks, I stretch so wide,
With petals bright, I take great pride.
My jokes may flop, but I don't fret,
For laughter lingers, you can bet!

"Why does my stem have a sore back?"
"Maybe it's all that leaning crack!"
My friends all laugh, we sway along,
In this bright world, we all belong.

Raindrops giggle as they fall,
A dance party's called, let's have a ball!
With every droplet, joy expands,
A chorus formed by leafy bands.

So join my shade, no frowning found,
In my green realm, good vibes abound.
With nature's cheer, I promise this,
Life's much more fun with a little bliss!

## The Gift of Soft Resilience

In a pot on my sill, quite a sight,
A plant claims the day, with roots tucked tight.
Its leaves stand tall, but when I poke,
They droop a bit, like a sleepy joke.

I water it gently, it gives me a grin,
Like it knows the secrets to life within.
A friend for the chaos, it sways to and fro,
Whispering wisdom that only we know.

Oh, my leafy buddy, so calm and so bright,
You wear a cool robe without a fright.
When life throws a tantrum, it seems to say,
"Don't worry, dear human, we'll be okay!"

Light-hearted and low, here's my tale's end,
This plant's just a perk, my unshakable friend.
In laughter we grow, in silliness bloom,
Together we dance, dispelling the gloom.

## A Soft Lullaby from Nature

A green little songbird sits on my desk,
No singing it does, oh, it's quite the jest!
With leaves like a blanket, it cuddles the air,
Whispering dreams without a care.

The sunlight creeps in, what a funny glare,
It tickles the plant and lifts up its hair.
As I sip my tea, I can't help but grin,
This sleepy green buddy keeps cozy within.

With petals so soft, and a sway to its tune,
It comforts the heart, like a whimsical rune.
"Just chillax," it seems to silently croon,
"Tomorrow's a day, with a bit more of noon!"

So here I sit, chuckling away,
With a plant that knows just how to play.
From roots to leaves, it's my comic relief,
In a world full of chaos, it brings me belief.

## **Sanctuary in Bloom**

In the corner, it stands, with a wink and a grin,
A sanctuary soft, where the laughter begins.
It doesn't do much, just lounges about,
But it surely knows how to keep worries out.

Dust motes are dancing, the sun's having fun,
My leafy companion, oh, how we have spun!
Tickling the air with its delicate ease,
It just leans back, as if saying, "Please!"

I talk to it daily, it never complains,
In its very green world, nothing's ever in chains.
With a twitch of a leaf, it lightens my day,
In this soft little oasis, we giggle and play.

So here's to the blooms with their whimsical cheer,
Bringing joy to the moments, making stress disappear.
Together we thrive, in this sanctuary bright,
Sharing a chuckle in the glow of the light.

## Unraveled Threads of Peace

Tangled up laughter, in a round woven pot,
This plant spins a tale that tickles a lot.
With leaves like a smile, it stretches out wide,
Embracing the chaos, as life's silly guide.

I've named it Sir Wobble, for reasons profound,
It nods at my jokes, the best friend I've found.
When life's threads unravel, it's joyous and spry,
With a sip of fresh water, it reaches for the sky.

In moments of quiet, when the day feels absurd,
I share all my secrets, not scared of a word.
It just sways and chuckles, in whispers and sighs,
This leafy companion sees through all the lies.

So here's to the greenery, the chuckle-filled leaves,
With softness that wraps like a cozy old sleeve.
In the fabric of laughter, we stitch and we mend,
Unraveled threads of peace, with my green little friend.

## Promises Woven in Leaf

In the sunny nook where I stand bright,
A plant with a grin, what a silly sight.
Whispers of hope in my verdant embrace,
Winking with joy, in this leafy space.

Soaking up sun with a laugh and a cheer,
I twist and I curl, weave your dreams here.
Each leaf a promise, oh what a delight,
Life's little giggles sparkle in the light.

Water me well, but don't drown my spunk,
I thrive on your love, not a soggy funk.
Trim my brown edges, I won't hold a grudge,
Just promise me laughter, I won't budge.

With petals a'plenty and roots aplenty too,
I promise to grow, with a wink and a woo.
So come sit beside me, join in my dance,
Together we'll thrive, give life a chance!

## Guardian of the Gentle Light

In a cozy corner, I keep watch with glee,
Guarding your peace, just you and me.
In each bright petal, a sparkle I hide,
A cheeky lil' friend, your good luck guide.

Dancing to sunlight, in my leafy attire,
I throw shade at worries, that's my desire.
Should gloom try to sneak in, I'll shake my leaves fast,
With a chuckle and spin, your troubles won't last.

Water me kindly, let the laughter flow,
I'll shimmer with joy like a leafy show.
If you tickle my roots, I might just giggle,
And together we'll dance, oh don't be so wiggle!

So here's to my promise, a bond light and bright,
I'll guard your heart, with delight in sight.
In this gentle space, we'll flourish and grow,
Just me and my light, putting on a show!

# Harmony in the Hidden

In a quiet nook where secrets reside,
Whispers of joy and giggles collide.
With leaves like canopies, I wear my crown,
In this leafy palace, I won't let you frown.

Sunshine tickles me, I laugh in return,
Each bloom a crafted delight, for you to learn.
Plant tricks and tales in the soil of your heart,
In this joyful chaos, we'll never part.

So remember my leaves, they dance with grace,
In every little wrinkle, there's a smiling face.
Life's quirky moments, we'll gather around,
With every new leaf, another laugh is found.

In this harmony hidden, together we'll soar,
With promises woven, always wanting more.
Just a wink from my petals, and you'll see the fun,
In this wild garden, we'll join as one!

## Echoes of a Pure Soul

In whispers of green, an echo resounds,
A chuckle, a wiggle, where joy abounds.
I wave as you pass, don't take it too slow,
My mission: to lighten your heart, you know!

With roots deep in kindness, I gather my glee,
In every soft leaf, a party for three.
Find laughter in petals, a twinkle in air,
With each little rustle, I promise to care.

So pluck away worries, let giggles abide,
With a sprinkle of sunshine, I flourish with pride.
In the dance of our days, we'll sway and we'll chat,
Echoes of laughter, where friendships are at.

Peace in my promise, a hush so divine,
In this garden of joy, your heart I entwine.
With every new bloom, our happiness grows,
What a delightful riddle, a life that glows!

## Light Filtering Through Green

Sunlight dances on my floor,
Leaves are giggling, wanting more.
A beam slips in, all bright and clean,
Whispering secrets of the green.

Dust bunnies wiggle in delight,
As foliage flaunts its leafy right.
They wear their shades to look so cool,
Sprouting laughter, nature's rule.

Squirrels peek through the window wide,
Chasing shadows, making me hide.
Each petal winks, they know the game,
In this green place, I'm never lame.

Joy blooms here with every sight,
Photosynthesis feels just right.
Plant puns echo, let's have some cheer,
In our leafy world, there's nothing to fear.

## **A Promise in Every Leaf**

A leaf espies with cheeky grace,
Hiding secrets in its space.
With every bloom, a giggle starts,
Nature knows how to win hearts.

Each stem struts like it's on parade,
Unfurling tales that never fade.
If leaves could talk, oh what they'd say,
About the mischief of the day!

Roots tap dance beneath the ground,
While earthworms shuffle all around.
Bubbles of laughter fill the air,
With each new sprout, without a care.

Sunbeams tickle leaves so light,
Nature's humor, pure delight.
So take a moment, just breathe in,
Join the revelry that's within.

## Whispers of a Quiet Heart

In the hush of shiny dew,
Whispers float as if they knew.
Petals giggle, swaying low,
They've got jokes, let's hear the show!

Quiet moments, plants do thrive,
As frogs leap and bees arrive.
Each heart thump echoes in the breeze,
Tickling branches with such ease.

Laughter bubbles, soft and round,
As nature's symphony resounds.
Frolicking roots make friends below,
As grasshoppers steal the show.

So pause and listen, let it start,
The tales of laughter from the heart.
In tranquility, joy does spark,
In whispers of the quiet park.

## The Embrace of Soft Shadows

Shadows play like playful sprites,
Dancing 'neath the leaf-lit lights.
They stretch and twist, a funny sight,
Giggling softly, day and night.

In the garden, there's a jest,
Bugs in costumes, oh what a fest!
Beetles roll in tiny races,
Finding cover in soft places.

The sun, a jester, casts its rays,
Turning leaves into bright displays.
Each shadow laughs as it departs,
In this theater of nature's arts.

So join the revelry, come along,
In the garden, we all belong.
With every sway and every cheer,
In soft shadows, joy is near!

**In the Garden of Whispered Promises**

In a garden where giggles grow,
Flowers dance in a row,
Rabbits wear hats and play chess,
While bugs bust moves in a colorful dress.

Petunias plotting their next hoedown,
With daisies spinning, never a frown,
Sunflowers take selfies, striking a pose,
Even the weeds can't help but doze.

Lettuce tells jokes about romaine,
Cabbage chuckles—what a silly strain!
With vegetables painting their leaves bright,
The garden's a riot of pure delight.

So come sip tea, hear the plants rap,
In this quirky world of leafy clap,
Where blossoms giggle and grasshoppers sing,
Nature's humor is the most charming thing.

## The Spirit of Gentle Renewal

At dawn, the dew drops giggle and play,
Waking up blooms in a comical way,
With petals dressed in the sunlight's best,
They reenact scenes from a flower fest.

The daisies quip about the bees' dance,
While hydrangeas join in with a chance,
To turn up the volume, a voice so grand,
"Don't step on us; we're part of the band!"

A butterfly winks with a dash of flair,
As it flutters past without a care,
"It's a party here, without a doubt,
Join in the fun, there's no need to pout!"

So let's celebrate each little sprout,
In this funny world where laughter's about,
Nature's renewal brings joy anew,
In every petal, there's humor too.

## Whispers of Tranquility

In the garden of whispers, plants conspire,
Telling secrets that never tire,
The ferns giggle, "We're the best at shade,"
While silly tulips throw a parade!

The sunflowers gossip about the clouds,
Comparing hats, both bright and loud,
Lilies float like they own the pond,
Making frogs feel a little less fond.

Amidst the blooms, the breeze chimes in,
Tickling petals, creating a spin,
Without a care, they dance without fears,
Swaying and laughing through joyful tears.

So come taste the laughter, it's on the vine,
Where even the thorns just want to dine,
In a realm where calm meets bubbly cheer,
Nature's wittiness is crystal clear.

## **Serenity in Bloom**

In a field where calm meets the jest,
Petals burst forth in an elegant quest,
Chasing butterflies, oh what a sight,
Everyone's laughing; what pure delight!

Roses share tales of their date with bees,
As tulips crack jokes in the gentle breeze,
Even the daisies are up for some fun,
Basking in glow of the warm morning sun.

Cacti wear shades, feeling so cool,
While pansies splash water, a playful pool,
Each bloom holds a giggle, a chuckle to spare,
In this riotous garden, love's in the air!

So let's join hands in this blooming affair,
Where laughter blossoms, without a care,
In a tapestry woven of amusing cheer,
Nature's humor is perfectly clear.

## Beneath the Gentle Veil

In a pot with a smile, she sways,
Her leaves dance around, oh what a craze!
Water me gently, but not too much,
Or I'll sulk in the corner, just out of touch.

With petals so bright, she makes quite the show,
Standing proud on my sill, where the sun likes to glow.
Some say I'm a green thumb, a bit of a pro,
But I just play it cool; she's the star of the show.

## Blooming in Quietude

In silence, she blooms, with a wink and a grin,
Proving the garden can rock with some spin.
Her colors so bold, they startle the bees,
Who land on her petals, as if they're at ease.

No noise in the night, just a leaf's gentle rustle,
She giggles in chlorophyll, quiet yet bustling.
I whisper my secrets, for she keeps them safe,
An undercover friend, in this floral space.

## The Heart's Gentle Offering

Here's a little bud, with charm so refined,
Always ready to cheer, an amazing find.
She nods as I talk, like she totally gets,
Every silly mishap and all of my frets.

With every new sprout, she teases the air,
"Oh darling, just chill, there's no need to scare!"
A therapist dressed in soft shades of green,
Making sure I'm happy, a real garden queen.

## A Symphony of Solitude

In my cozy nook, she plays solo tunes,
Her leaves strumming softly beneath the full moons.
With a flick and a flap, she brings forth delight,
Turning my evenings from dull into bright.

She hums with the breeze, sharing gossip so sweet,
"No drama around here, just a calm little beat."
It's a party for one, but she doesn't complain,
In our leafy duet, peace flows like a refrain.

www.ingramcontent.com/pod-product-compliance
Lightning Source LLC
Chambersburg PA
CBHW070334120526
44590CB00017B/2873